The Chord Son
stereoph.....

Wise Publications
London/New York/Sydney/Paris/Copenhagen/Madrid

Exclusive Distributors:

Music Sales Limited
8/9 Frith Street,
London W1V 5TZ, England.
Music Sales Pty Limited
120 Rothschild Avenue,
Rosebery, NSW 2018, Australia.

Order No. AM956065
ISBN 0-7119-7444-6
This book © Copyright 1999 by Wise Publications

Compiled by Peter Evans
Music arranged by Rikky Rooksby
Music processed by The Pitts

Printed in the United Kingdom by
Caligraving Limited, Thetford, Norfolk.

Your Guarantee of Quality
As publishers, we strive to produce every book
to the highest commercial standards.
This book has been carefully designed to minimise awkward
page turns and to make playing from it a real pleasure.
Particular care has been given to specifying acid-free,
neutral-sized paper made from pulps which have not been
elemental chlorine bleached. This pulp is from farmed sustainable
forests and was produced with special regard for the environment.
Throughout, the printing and binding have been planned to
ensure a sturdy, attractive publication which should give years
of enjoyment. If your copy fails to meet our high standards,
please inform us and we will gladly replace it.

Music Sales' complete catalogue describes thousands
of titles and is available in full colour sections by subject,
direct from Music Sales Limited. Please state your areas of interest
and send a cheque/postal order for £1.50 for postage to:
Music Sales Limited, Newmarket Road,
Bury St. Edmunds, Suffolk IP33 3YB.

Relative Tuning

The guitar can be tuned with the aid of pitch pipes or dedicated electronic guitar tuners which are available through your local music dealer. If you do not have a tuning device, you can use relative tuning. Estimate the pitch of the 6th string as near as possible to E or at least a comfortable pitch (not too high, as you might break other strings in tuning up). Then, while checking the various positions on the diagram, place a finger from your left hand on the:

5th fret of the E or 6th string and **tune the open A** (or 5th string) to the note Ⓐ

5th fret of the A or 5th string and **tune the open D** (or 4th string) to the note Ⓓ

5th fret of the D or 4th string and **tune the open G** (or 3rd string) to the note Ⓖ

4th fret of the G or 3rd string and **tune the open B** (or 2nd string) to the note Ⓑ

5th fret of the B or 2nd string and **tune the open E** (or 1st string) to the note Ⓔ

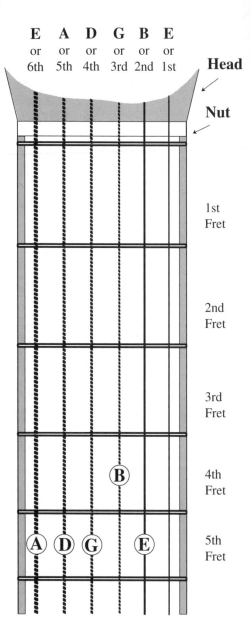

Reading Chord Boxes

Chord boxes are diagrams of the guitar neck viewed head upwards, face on as illustrated. The top horizontal line is the nut, unless a higher fret number is indicated, the others are the frets.

The vertical lines are the strings, starting from E (or 6th) on the left to E (or 1st) on the right.

The black dots indicate where to place your fingers.

Strings marked with an O are played open, not fretted.

Strings marked with an X should not be played.

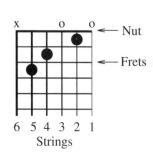

4

A Thousand Trees

Words by Kelly Jones
Music by Kelly Jones, Richard Jones & Stuart Cable

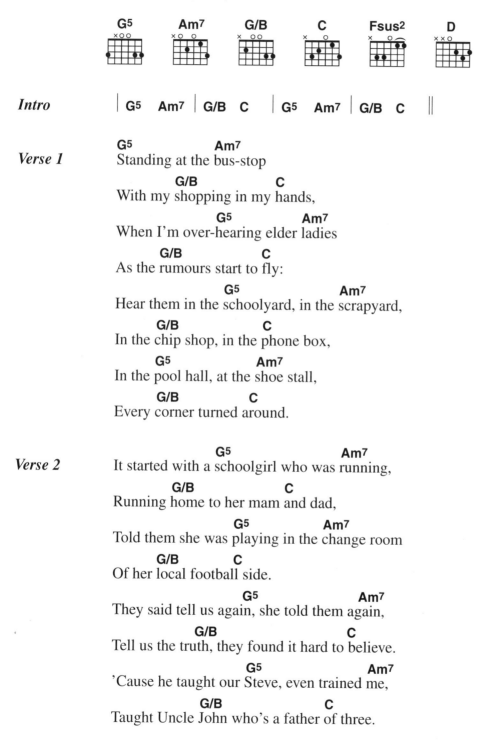

Intro | G5   Am7 | G/B   C | G5   Am7 | G/B   C ||

Verse 1

G5   Am7
Standing at the bus-stop

        G/B   C
With my shopping in my hands,

           G5   Am7
When I'm over-hearing elder ladies

        G/B   C
As the rumours start to fly:

           G5   Am7
Hear them in the schoolyard, in the scrapyard,

        G/B   C
In the chip shop, in the phone box,

        G5   Am7
In the pool hall, at the shoe stall,

        G/B   C
Every corner turned around.

Verse 2

           G5   Am7
It started with a schoolgirl who was running,

        G/B   C
Running home to her mam and dad,

           G5   Am7
Told them she was playing in the change room

        G/B   C
Of her local football side.

           G5   Am7
They said tell us again, she told them again,

        G/B   C
Tell us the truth, they found it hard to believe.

           G5   Am7
'Cause he taught our Steve, even trained me,

        G/B   C
Taught Uncle John who's a father of three.

Chorus 1

        Am⁷   **Fsus²**   **C**
Only takes one tree to make a thousand matches,

        Am⁷   **Fsus² C**   **G⁵** **Am⁷ G/B C**
Only takes one match to burn a thousand ____ trees,

    G⁵   **Am⁷ G/B C**
Thousand trees. ____

Verse 3

       G⁵   **Am⁷**
See it in the classroom or the swimming pool

      G/B   **C**
Where the matchstick men are made.

    G⁵   **Am⁷**
At the Scouts' hall, at the football,

      G/B   **C**
Where the wise we trust are paid.

        G⁵   **Am⁷**
They all honour his name, did a lot for the game,

      G/B   **C**
He had his name knocked up above the sports ground gates.

      G⁵   **Am⁷**
Now they're ripping them down, stamping the ground.

G/B   **C**
Picture gathers dust in the bar in the lounge.

Chorus 2

        Am⁷   **Fsus²**   **C**
It takes one tree to make a thousand matches,

        Am⁷   **Fsus² C**   **G⁵** **Am⁷ G/B C**
Only takes one match to burn a thousand ____ trees,

    G⁵   **Am⁷ G/B C**
Thousand trees. ____

Bridge

D   **Fsus²**   **C**
Wake up, smell the rain.

D   **Fsus² C**
Shake up, he's back to stay.

D   **Fsus² C**
Hasn't been on a holi - day,

D   **Fsus²**   **C**
Growing seeds don't believe why he's

G⁵ **Am⁷**   **G/B C**
Been __ a - way. ____

Link

‖: **G⁵** **Am⁷** | **G/B C** :‖ *Play 3 times*

Verse 4

      G5   **Am7**
In the schoolyard, change room,

G/B   **C**
Playing fields, bathroom,

G5   **Am7**
Phone box, office blocks,

G/B   **C**
Corners turned around.

             G5   **Am7**
They keep doubting the flame, tossing the blame.

    G/B   **C**
Got his name knocked up above the sports ground gates,

      G5   **Am7**
Now they're ripping them down, stamping the ground,

G/B   **C**
Picture gathers dust in the bar in the lounge.

Chorus 3

   Am7   **Fsus2**   **C**
It takes one tree to make a thousand matches,

    Am7   **Fsus2 C**   **G5** **Am7** **G/B** **C**
Only takes one match to burn a thousand _____ trees,

   G5 **Am7** **G/B** **C**
Thousand trees, _____

   G5 **Am7** **G/B** **C**
Thousand trees, _____

   G5 **Am7** **G/B** **C**
Thousand _____ trees. _____

A Minute Longer

Words by Kelly Jones
Music by Kelly Jones, Richard Jones & Stuart Cable

D Em G Em7 Bm7 G* A7 A7sus4

Intro | D | Em | G | D ||

Verse 1
                  D   **Em**
They're calling out, come on let's go,
   G   **D**
But I'm miles away to a year before:
                      Em
Laughs from a glass, drank to the past,
      G   **Em**   **G**
On the old green seat like velvet to the hand. _____

Chorus 1
D   **Em7**   **G**
  Think I'd like to stay a minute longer _____
D   **Em7**   **G**
  Would you like to stay a minute longer? _____

Verse 2
                D   **Em**
Last one for some, sick from the rum,
  G   **D**
I played golf on the carpet with someone.
                   Em
Crash back to date, few things I hate,
      G   **Em** **G**
But I'd rather us live in the present day. _____

Chorus 2
D   **Em7**   **G**
  Think I'd like to stay a minute longer _____
D   **Em7**   **G**
  Would you like to stay a minute longer? _____

Middle

Bm7   **G***
Hey, _____ aah. _____

Bm7   **G***
Hey, _____ aah. _____

Bm7   **G***
Hey, _____ aah. _____

A7 **A7sus4** **A7**
Aah. _____

Chorus 3

D   **Em7**   **G**
 Think I'd like to stay a minute longer _____

D   **Em7** **G**
 Would you like to stay a minute longer? _____

Chorus 4

D   **Em7**   **G**
 If you like I'd stay a minute longer,

D   **Em7**   **G**
 If you like I'd stay a minute longer.

   D Em7 **G**
It's longer, it's longer,

   D **Em7** **G Em7** **G** **D**
Longer, it's longer.

Billy Daveys Daughter

Words by Kelly Jones
Music by Kelly Jones, Richard Jones & Stuart Cable

| Csus2 | Em | G | C | D/F# | Em7 | Am | D |

Intro | Csus2 | Csus2 | Em | Em | G | G |

| C | C | G | G D/F# ‖

Verse 1

Em7   G
I never knew her __ name,

C   G
I only knew her __ fame.

Em7   G
She lived near my __ town,

C   G   D/F#
Another goldfish to drown. __

Pre-chorus

Em7   G
Well, I just passed the bridge

C   G   D/F#
That parts us from __ them,

Em7   G
The bridge that she __ used

C   Am7 C
Again and again, __ again.

Chorus 1

G   D
I remember when they found her,

C
Billy Davey's daughter.

   G D/F# C
The word gets around,

   G D/F# C
The word gets around.

Chorus 2

G
Billy Davey's second daughter

D/F♯
Threw herself to dirty water,

C
Billy's left with nothing

     D
But a ___ dream.

Chorus 3

G
Billy Davey's second daughter

D/F♯
Threw herself to dirty water,

C
Billy's left with nothing

     D
But a ___ dream.

Outro

    G   **D/F♯**
He dreams, he dreams,

C   **D**
Dreams, dreams.

    G   **D/F♯**
He dreams, he dreams,

C   **D**
Dreams, dreams.

G   **D/F♯** **C**   **G**
Word gets around.

Goldfish Bowl

Words by Kelly Jones
Music by Kelly Jones, Richard Jones & Stuart Cable

G   D   C   Bm⁷   Em⁷   Cadd⁹

Verse 1

    G   D   C
Same long faces in the work-mans' hall,

    G   D   C
Caramel crisp counts his birds, __

    G   D   C
Cliff chips lines up his dominoes,

    G   D   C
Kingfisher lead singer calms his nerves. __

Chorus 1

Bm⁷   C   Bm⁷
I'm drinking, sinking, swimming and drowning,

           C   Bm⁷
Working, smirking, learning and burning,

          C   D
Sleeping, thieving, cheating, beating,

                    G
I'm eating, I'm deep in a goldfish   bowl.

D   C
It's sink or swim.

Verse 2

    G   D   C
The hall downtown just burned to the ground,

    G   D   C
My boxing ring turned to ash.

    G   D   C
Red-head gingerbread sells tickets at the door,

    G   D   C
Stella sleepwalks in the sand.

Chorus 2

Bm⁷   C   Bm⁷
I'm drinking, sinking, swimming and drowning,

              C   Bm⁷
Working, smirking, learning and burning,

              C   D
Sleeping, thieving, cheating, beating,

                                   G
I'm eating, I'm deep in a goldfish   bowl.

D   C
It's sink or swim.

                G
They're lookin' in,

D   C
They're lookin' in. ____

Solo

‖: D | Em⁷ | Cadd⁹ | Cadd⁹   :‖

Verse 3

G   D   C
Hard up, outta luck, time to ride the village bike,

G   D   C
A bike been used ten times or more.

G   D   C
Grapevine, here's the wife, lays down her royal flush,

G   D   C
I think I've lost another __ wife.

Chorus 3

Bm⁷   C   Bm⁷
I'm drinking, sinking, swimming and drowning,

              C   Bm⁷
Working, smirking, learning and burning,

              C   D
Sleeping, thieving, cheating, beating,

                                   G
I'm eating, I'm deep in a goldfish   bowl.

D   C
It's sink or swim.

                G
They're lookin' in,

D   C   G
It's sink or swim.

Half The Lies You Tell Ain't True

Words by Kelly Jones
Music by Kelly Jones, Richard Jones & Stuart Cable

G5   B5   Gsus2   G5/F♯   A5   D5   E5

Intro | N.C. (G5) | (G5) |

Verse 1

B5   G5 Gsus2
  You could lick or chew, tongue in style tonight, _____

B5   G5
  Champagne drag-queen suit, pinstripe out-ta line, _____

  G5/F♯
It's time to try.

B5   G5 Gsus2
  Blisters on your feet, blisters up your spine, _____

B5
  If I could choose from two,

       G5 G5/F♯
I'd mime to be a smile, ha ha ha ha.

Chorus 1

A5
  But when you rely on a lie that's true,

No-one believes in the things you do,

               B5
'Cause half of the lies you tell ain't true.

     D5
I'm gonna find out,

B5   D5
  I'm gonna find a piece of…

Verse 2

        B5   G5   Gsus2

You could pick and lose, diesel dream for crime, _____

B5   G5   G5/F♯

I should win and choose, colours undersize, a naked fake that's

B5

Face that fits for two.

                 G5   Gsus2

Sex brings out the spies _____

B5   G5   G5/F♯

Hanging from your feet, Hollywood star style, ha ha ha ha.

Chorus 2

A5

But when you rely on a lie that's true,

No-one believes in the things you do,

                              B5

'Cause half of the lies you tell ain't true.

        D5

I'm gonna find out,

B5   D5

I'm gonna find a piece of…

Middle

| E5 | E5 | E5 | E5 | |

You.

| E5 | E5 | E5 | E5 | ||

Chorus 3

A5

But when you rely on a lie that's true,

No-one believes in the things you do.

                              B5

'Cause half of the lies you tell ain't true.

        D5

I'm gonna find a piece of you.

Chorus 4

A5

But when you rely on a lie that's true,

No-one believes in the things you do,

                              B5

'Cause half of the lies you tell ain't true.

        D5   B5   D5

I'm gonna find out, I'm gonna find out,

B5   D5   A5

I'm gonna find a piece of you.

Hurry Up And Wait

Words by Kelly Jones
Music by Kelly Jones, Richard Jones & Stuart Cable

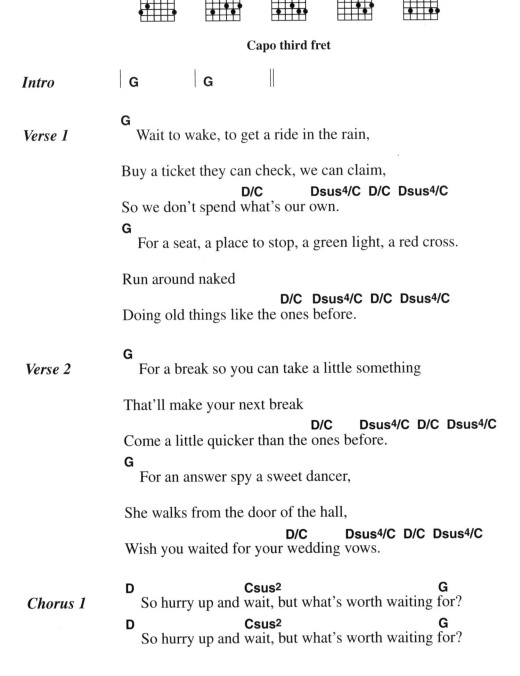

G   D/C   Dsus4/C   D   Csus2

Capo third fret

Intro | G | G ||

Verse 1
G
 Wait to wake, to get a ride in the rain,

Buy a ticket they can check, we can claim,
            D/C   Dsus4/C D/C Dsus4/C
So we don't spend what's our own.
G
 For a seat, a place to stop, a green light, a red cross.

Run around naked
                    D/C Dsus4/C D/C Dsus4/C
Doing old things like the ones before.

Verse 2
G
 For a break so you can take a little something

That'll make your next break
                  D/C   Dsus4/C D/C Dsus4/C
Come a little quicker than the ones before.
G
 For an answer spy a sweet dancer,

She walks from the door of the hall,
                 D/C   Dsus4/C D/C Dsus4/C
Wish you waited for your wedding vows.

Chorus 1
D   Csus2   G
 So hurry up and wait, but what's worth waiting for?
D   Csus2   G
 So hurry up and wait, but what's worth waiting for?

Verse 3

G
We wait to get warm, the car starts from cold,

Stall to make a first move
                              D/C   **Dsus⁴/C D/C Dsus⁴/C**
Magazines made the rules to make us lose.
G
  For your dream man,

The house you could both plan, the car in the sales ad,

The wet dream
                        D/C   **Dsus⁴/C D/C Dsus⁴/C**
With the man you wish that you had.

Chorus 2   As Chorus 1

Verse 4

G
  A watched pot never boils, sugar seconds to dissolve,

Feel your appetite loss,
                        D/C   **Dsus⁴/C D/C Dsus⁴/C**
Food's relevance   lost inside.
G
  We wait to get there, and when we get there we wait around
                                        D/C   **Dsus⁴/C D/C Dsus⁴/C**
For anyone to tell us what we even got there for.

Chorus 3   As Chorus 1

Chorus 4

Csus²   **G   Csus²**   **G**
  What's worth waiting for?   What's worth waiting for?
Csus²   **G**   **Csus²**
  What's worth waiting for? _____
                                G
What's worth waiting for?

Coda

G
  So join the queue, me and you, wait in line,
                              D/C Dsus⁴/C D/C Dsus⁴/C
It takes our time to be satisfied, _____

        G   **Csus²**
‖: i - i - ied, i - ied, ___ :‖   *Repeat to fade*

17

I Stopped To Fill My Car Up

Words by Kelly Jones
Music by Kelly Jones, Richard Jones & Stuart Cable

Am   Em/G   F   C   G/B   C/G   Fsus2   Em7

Intro

| Am Em/G | F | Am Em/G | F   ‖

Verse 1

Am   Em/G F
I stopped to fill my car up.

Am   Em/G   F
The car felt   good that   day.

Am   Em/G   F
I didn't know where I was going

Am   Em/G   F
But it felt good for a   change.

Am   Em/G   F
A five and a pocket full of silver,

Am   Em/G   F
I paid the lady, no   change,

Am   Em/G   F
And then it started to piss down,

Am   Em/G   F
I started drivin' again.

Chorus 1

C   G/B
And then I looked up

        Am   C/G   F
And looked in the mirror behind me.

C   G/B
And then I looked up

        Am   C/G   F   Fsus2 F Fsus2
And looked in the mirror behind me. _____

Verse 2

    Am   Em/G   F
A man round forty in the back-seat

    Am   Em/G   F
Must have stepped in when I was empty.

    Am   Em/G   F
So why's he sat there just waiting,

    Am   Em/G   F
Likely to smash my face in.

    Am   Em/G   F
He had a bag full of money,

    Am   Em/G   F
He said just drive me away.

    Am   Em/G   F
I didn't know where I was going,

    Am Em/G   F
Yet it felt good to be strange.

Chorus 2

    C   G/B
And still I look up

        Am   C/G   F
And look in the mirror behind me.

    C   G/B
And still I look up

        Am   C/G   F   Fsus2 F Fsus2
And look in the mirror behind me. _____

Verse 3

    Am   Em/G F
Curiosity is over,

    Am   Em/G   F
He stepped down from the car.

    Am   Em/G   F
He pulled a gun from his jacket,

    Am   Em7   F
Said I was going to die.

    Am   Em/G   F
It gives me so much satisfaction

    Am   Em/G   F
To watch you   beg and   cry,

    Am   Em/G   F
Well I just made up this story

    Am   Em/G   F
To get your attention, makes me   smile.

Chorus 3

    C   G/B   Am   C/G   F   Fsus2
I never looked up or looked in the mirror behind me.

    C   G/B   Am   C/G   F
I never looked up or looked in the mirror behind me.

I Wouldn't Believe Your Radio

Words by Kelly Jones
Music by Kelly Jones, Richard Jones & Stuart Cable

Aadd9   Cmaj7   G6   D   C   G   Em7   A7sus4

Intro

| Drums for 4 bars ‖: Asus2 | Asus2 | Cmaj7 | G6 :‖

Verse 1

Aadd9   Cmaj7   G6
Travelling through a tunnel under sea,
Aadd9
You never know if it cracks in half,
    Cmaj7   G6
You're never ever gonna see me.

Chorus 1

D   C   G
But you can have it all if you like,
D   C   G
You can have it all if you like,

And you can pay for it the rest of your
Aadd9   Cmaj7   G6
Li - -   fe,
Aadd9   Cmaj7   G6
Li - -   fe.

Verse 2

Aadd9   Cmaj7   G6
I wouldn't believe your wireless radio.
Aadd9
If I had myself a flying giraffe
    Cmaj7   G6
You'd have one in a box with a window.

Chorus 2   As Chorus 1

Solo   ‖: D | C | G | G :‖

Middle

    Em7   A7sus4   Em7
      Life in the summer's on its back,

                    A7sus4   Em7
  You'd have to agree that that's the crack,

                 A7sus4   G
  So take what you want, I'm not coming back.

Chorus 3

    D   C   G
      So you can have it all if you like,

    D   C   G
    You can have it all if you like,

    D   C   G
      So you can have it all if you like,

    D   C   G
    You can have it all if you like,

                                     Aadd9
  And you can pay for it the rest of your

            Cmaj7 G6
  Li -   -   fe,

  Aadd9 Cmaj7 G6
  Li -   -   fe,

  Aadd9 Cmaj7 G6
  Li -   -   fe,

  Aadd9 Cmaj7 G6
  Li -   -   fe.

Coda

‖: Aadd9 | Aadd9 G6 | Aadd9 | Aadd9 G6 :‖ Aadd9 ‖

Is Yesterday, Tomorrow, Today?

Words by Kelly Jones
Music by Kelly Jones, Richard Jones & Stuart Cable

A	D	Bm7	E/G♯	A/C♯	Gadd9

Intro ‖ A | D | A | D ‖

Verse 1

A   D   A
It's another way to get through the day,

              D   A
Pickin' up ripped cigarette boxes hoping that one remains,

           D   A
Yellow lucky day, suck deep and bathe

        D   Bm7
For the next ten minutes spent coughing all the pleasures craved.

Chorus 1

(Bm7)   A
Write down all the things that you'd like to say,

Bm7   A   E/G♯ A
Write down all the things that you'd like to change,

Bm7   A
Write down all the places you'd like to stay,

Bm7
Write down anything that you want.

D   A
Is yesterday, tomorrow, today?

     Bm7   A   Bm7
Hey, hey, is nothing gonna change the way? Hey, hey.

Verse 2

N.C.   A   D   A
Cracked rock top wall, left ash to fall, left alone to wait,

        D   A
I've never looked at things, I've liked only things I hate.

          D   A
You're not the first today, not the softest face,

        D   Bm7
Was there any that you liked, was there any that you didn't fake?

Chorus 2

(Bm7)   A
Write down all the things that you'd like to be,

Bm7   A   E/G♯ A
Write down all the things that you don't believe, ___

Bm7   A
Write down all the places you'd like to see,

Bm7
Write down anything that you want.

    D   A   Bm7
Is yesterday, tomorrow, today? ___

                      A   Bm7
Is nothing gonna change the way, hey?

Bridge

        A/C♯ D   E
'Cause every-thing that's you,

          A/C♯   D   E
And the things that you like to do,

      A/C♯   D   E
And all of the things that are,

      Bm7
Come back again,

      Gadd9   A   D
Come back   again, ___

          A   D
Come back again, ___

          A   D
Come back again, ___

          A   D
Come back again. ___

    Gadd9
Is yesterday, tomorrow, to-(day?)

Coda

A	D	A	D	

-day?

| Bm7 | Gadd9 | Bm7 | Gadd9 | A | ‖ |

23

Just Looking

Words by Kelly Jones
Music by Kelly Jones, Richard Jones & Stuart Cable

G   C   Am7   Fsus2   G5

Cadd9   D*   Em   D/F#   A5

Intro   ‖: G | G | C | C :‖

Verse 1
                     G   C
There's things I want, there's things I think I want,
                   G   C
There's things I've had, there's things I wanna have.
           Am7   Fsus2
Do I want the   dreams, the ones we're   forced to see?

Verse 2
                       G   C
Do I want the perfect   wife, the word 'perfect'   ain't quite right.
                 G   C
Shoppin' every day, take it back the next break.
           Am7   Fsus2
They say the more you fly the more you risk your life.

Chorus 1
                 G5   Cadd9   G5   Cadd9
And I'm just look - in', I'm not buy - in',
           G5   Cadd9   G5   Cadd9
I'm just look - in', it keeps me smil - in'.

Verse 3
                       G   C
A house I seen, another   coulda' been.
                   G   C
You drenched my   head and I said what I said.
           Am7   Fsus2
Said that life is what you make of it yet most of us just fake.

Chorus 2   As Chorus 1

Link

| C | D* | C | D* | |

| C | D* | Em D/F♯ | G5 A5 | |

Chorus 3

          G5   Cadd9   G5   Cadd9
And I'm just look - in', I'm not buy - in',

          G5   Cadd9   G5   Cadd9
I'm just look - in', it keeps me try - in'.

          G5   Cadd9
And I'm just look - in', I'm not buy - in',

          G5   Cadd9   G5   Cadd9
I'm just look - in', it keeps me smil - in'.

Verse 4

                    G   C
There's things I   want, there's things I   think I want,

                    G   C
There's things I've   had, there's things I   wanna have.

              Am7   Fsus2
They say the more you fly the more you risk your life.

Coda

          G5   Cadd9   G5   Cadd9
But I'm just look - in', I'm not buy - in',

          G5   Cadd9   G5   Cadd9
I'm just look - in', keeps me smil - in'.

Last Of The Big Time Drinkers

Words by Kelly Jones
Music by Kelly Jones, Richard Jones & Stuart Cable

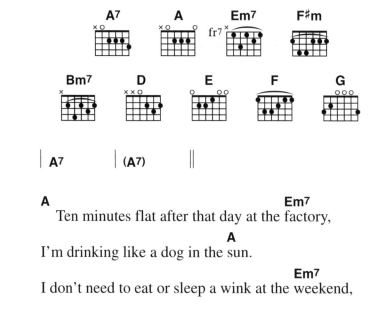

Intro　　　| **A7**　　　| **(A7)**　　　‖

Verse 1

　　　　　　　A　　　　　　　　　　　　　　　　　　**Em7**
　　　Ten minutes flat after that day at the factory,

　　　　　　　　　　　　　　　　　A
　　I'm drinking like a dog in the sun.

　　　　　　　　　　　　　　　　　　　　　　Em7
　　I don't need to eat or sleep a wink at the weekend,

　　Just rot my guts.

Pre-chorus 1

　　　　　F♯m　　　　　**Bm7**
　　And I can't wait for my next drink,

　　　　　F♯m　　　**D**
　　The first one is gonna sink.

Chorus 1

　　　　　　　　N.C.　　　　**A**　　　**E**
　　I'm the last of the big time drink-ers,

　　　　　Bm7
　　I take pride in my work.

　　　　　　　　E　　　　　　　**A**　　　**E**
　　I'm the last of the big time drink-ers,

　　　　　F
　　The beer don't taste the same

　　　　　G　　　　　　　　　　**D**　　　**F G**
　　Without my name painted on my glass.

Verse 2

A   Em⁷

I don't live to work, I work to live, live at the weekend,

                             A

And maybe spend a week in the sun.

                                         Em⁷

I come home, wet the bed, throw my sheets out the window

And Sunday morning comes and…

Pre-chorus 2   As Pre-chorus 1

Chorus 2   As Chorus 1

Solo   ‖: A | A | Em⁷ | Em⁷   :‖

Pre-chorus 3   As Pre-chorus 1

Chorus 3

(D)   A   E

I'm the last of the big time drink-ers,

         Bm⁷

I take pride in my work.

            E   A   E

I'm the last of the big time drink-ers,

            Bm⁷

Just gimme hops or the slops.

            E   A   E

I'm the last of the big time drink-ers,

         Bm⁷

I take pride in my work.

            E   A   E

I'm the last of the big time drink-ers,

F   G

Naah - naah.

Coda   ‖: A | A | Em⁷ | Em⁷   :‖   *Repeat to fade*

Local Boy In The Photograph

Words by Kelly Jones
Music by Kelly Jones, Richard Jones & Stuart Cable

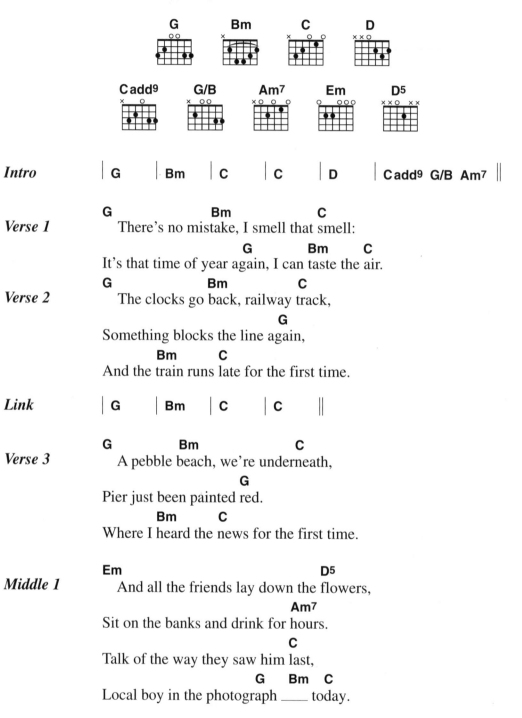

Intro | G | Bm | C | C | D | Cadd9 G/B Am7 ‖

Verse 1
> G   Bm   C
> There's no mistake, I smell that smell:
>   G   Bm   C
> It's that time of year again, I can taste the air.

Verse 2
> G   Bm   C
> The clocks go back, railway track,
>   G
> Something blocks the line again,
>   Bm   C
> And the train runs late for the first time.

Link | G | Bm | C | C | ‖

Verse 3
> G   Bm   C
> A pebble beach, we're underneath,
>   G
> Pier just been painted red.
>   Bm   C
> Where I heard the news for the first time.

Middle 1
> Em   D5
> And all the friends lay down the flowers,
>   Am7
> Sit on the banks and drink for hours.
>   C
> Talk of the way they saw him last,
>   G   Bm   C
> Local boy in the photograph ___ today.

Verse 4

G   Bm   C
   He'll always be twenty-three,

                         G
Yet the train runs on and on,

     Bm   C   D
Past the place they found his clothing.

   Cadd9 G/B   Cadd9 D   Cadd9 G/B
A bye - bye - bye - bye - bye,

Cadd9 D   Cadd9 G/B
Bye - bye - bye.

Cadd9 D   Cadd9 G/B Am7
Bye,   bye. _____

Verse 5

G   Bm   C
   There's no mistake, I smell that smell,

                      G
It's that time of year again.

     Bm   C
I can taste the air.

Verse 6

G   Bm   C
   The clocks go back, railway track,

                     G
Something blocks the line again.

     Bm   C   D   Cadd9 G/B Cadd9
And the train runs late for the first time today.

Middle 2

Em   D5
   And all the friends lay down the flowers,

                        Am7
Sit on the banks and drink for hours.

                        C
Talk of the way they saw him last,

                  G   Bm   C
Local boy in the photograph ___ today.

             G   Bm   C
He's going away.

Coda

| D | Cadd9 G/B Cadd9 | D | Cadd9 G/B Cadd9 |

| D | Cadd9 G/B Am7 | G   ‖

29

Looks Like Chaplin

Words by Kelly Jones
Music by Kelly Jones, Richard Jones & Stuart Cable

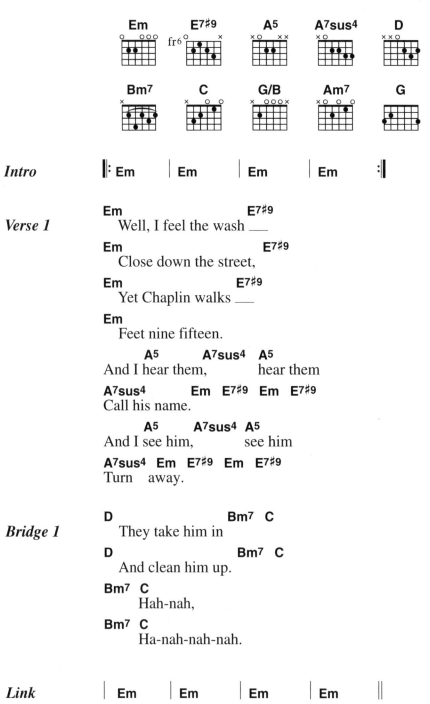

Intro   ‖: Em | Em | Em | Em :‖

Verse 1

Em   E7♯9
    Well, I feel the wash ___

Em   E7♯9
    Close down the street,

Em   E7♯9
    Yet Chaplin walks ___

Em
    Feet nine fifteen.

        A5   A7sus4   A5
And I hear them,   hear them

A7sus4   Em   E7♯9   Em   E7♯9
Call his name.

        A5   A7sus4   A5
And I see him,   see him

A7sus4   Em   E7♯9   Em   E7♯9
Turn   away.

Bridge 1

D   Bm7   C
    They take him in

D   Bm7   C
    And clean him up.

Bm7   C
    Hah-nah,

Bm7   C
    Ha-nah-nah-nah.

Link | Em | Em | Em | Em ‖

Verse 2

Em   E7♯9
   They take him in

Em   E7♯9
   And strip him down,

Em   E7♯9
   They dry his skin

Em
   And feed him wine,

      A5   A7sus4   A5
And I hear them,   hear them

A7sus4   Em   E7♯9   Em   E7♯9
Call his name.

      A5   A7sus4   A5
And I see him,   see him

A7sus4   Em   E7♯9   Em   E7♯9
Turn   away.

Bridge 2

D   Bm7   C
   Asks to use the phone,

D
   Yet he lives alone,

          Bm7
He lives alone,   there's no one,

C   G/B   Am7   G   D
No   one   home to   phone.

C   G/B   Am7   G   D
Sits   a   -   lone   at   home,

    C   G/B   Am7   G   D
He calls his   home his   own,

    C   G/B   Am7   G   D
His wife is   still   un - known.

More Life In A Tramps Vest

Words by Kelly Jones
Music by Kelly Jones, Richard Jones & Stuart Cable

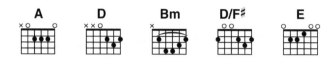

Intro

  A   **D**
I get camping eyes in the final hour,

            Bm
Last minute shoppers picking cauliflower,

The fuss they make,

  D   **A**
You'd swear they were buying a car.

Verse 1

 (A)   **D**
They always moan, moan it's not so cheap,

         Bm
Cheaper still, cheaper still down the street,

        D   **A**
Lose my rag and tell them, "Take your bag and shop down there."

           D
Closing down, they're closing down another road,

        Bm
One-way system steals the show,

      D
Mac the Knife swigs a can and sings the day away.

Chorus 1

    A
There's more life, more life, more life

   D/F♯   **E**
(Ah) in a tramp's vest.

    A
There's more life, more life, more life

   D/F♯   **E**
(Ah) in a tramp's vest.

Verse 2

      A   D
The flower man sits down in the street

                                             Bm
Surrounded by stock he bought back last week.

                      D   A
Bring back the ladies wearing lipstick on their teeth.

                              D
Make up, we make up a crappy joke,

                     Bm
Sit back, relax and have a smoke.

                    D
Mac the Knife swigs a can and sings the day away.

Chorus 2   As Chorus 1

Chorus 3   As Chorus 1

Solo | A | A | D | D | Bm | D ||

Tag

      A   D
I get camping eyes in the final hour,

                               Bm
Last minute shoppers picking cauliflower,

                    D
Mac the Knife swigs a can and sings the day away.

Chorus 4   As Chorus 1

Chorus 5

               A
There's more life, more life, more life

              D/F♯   E
(Ah) in a tramp's vest.

               A
There's more life, more life, more life

              D/F♯   E   A
(Ah) in a tramp's vest.

33

Not Up To You

Words by Kelly Jones
Music by Kelly Jones, Richard Jones & Stuart Cable

C5add9 G5 D/F♯ Em7 Am7 Bm7 Dsus4 D

Intro   ‖: C5add9 | C5add9 | G5 | G5 :‖

Verse 1

C5add9   G5
   Salt grips the road, awaits his lift again.

C5add9   G5
   Street orange glow shades the odds against.

C5add9   G5
   One more sip, a shoe, a miss,

                                C5add9
   A shaving nick, one extra kiss

   Who's to know, whatever!

Chorus 1

G5   D/F♯   Em7   C5add9
   Not up to me, not up to you.

G5   D/F♯   Em7
   Not up to me, not up to you.

Verse 2

C5add9   G5
   The swings don't swing, the park's been dead for years,

C5add9   G5
   How do you know your last swing was the last for good?

C5add9   G5
   Hard book on freaks, fresh summer peach,

                                     C5add9
   Creased magazine, sugared chocolate treat,

   Who's to know, whatever!

Chorus 2   As Chorus 1

Instrumental	Am7	Am7	Bm7	Bm7	Am7	Am7	

	Bm7	C5add9	Dsus4 D	D	D	D	‖

Verse 3

C5add9   G5
 The street's so long where she lost her pocket purse,

C5add9   G5
 Kept the last picture of the man she committed first.

C5add9   Em7
 Cracked windscreen rain, French murder play,

           Am7
Junk take-away, tired street parade,

           C5add9
Who's to know whatever, ____ ha, whatever.

Chorus 3

G5   D/F♯   Em7
 Not up to me, not up to you.

G5   D/F♯   Em7   C5add9
 Not up to me, not up to you, oh, whatever.

G5   D/F♯   Em7
 Not up to me, not up to you,

      C5add9 G5
Not up to anything we do.

     D/F♯   Em7   C5add9
Not up to me, not up to _____

   G5   D/F♯ Em7
Ha you, ha you, ha you.

    C5add9 G5
It's not up to   me,

D/F♯   Em7
 It's not up to you.

Link

	C5add9	C5add9	G5	‖

G5   C5add9
 It's not up to you,

G5   C5add9
 It's not up to you,

G5   C5add9
 It's not up to you. *Fade out*

Pick A Part That's New

Words by Kelly Jones
Music by Kelly Jones, Richard Jones & Stuart Cable

A   D   E   Asus2   Dsus2   Dm6   Dm

Intro | A | D | A | D |

| A | D | E | E D   ‖

Verse 1

Asus2
　I've never been here before,
　　　　　　　　Dsus2
Didn't know where to go,

Never met you before.
Asus2
　I've never been to your home,
　　　　　　　Dsus2
That smell's not unknown,
　　　　　　　　E
Footsteps made of stone.
　　　　　　　　D
Walking feels familiar.

Chorus 1

Asus2　　　　　　　　Dsus2
　You can do all the things that you'll like to do,
Asus2　　　　　　　　Dsus2
　All around, underground, pick a part that's new.
Asus2　　　　　　　　Dsus2
　You can do all the things that you'll like to do,
Asus2　　　　　　　　Dsus2　　　　E　　　　D
　All around, upside down, pick a part that's new.

Verse 2

Asus²
People drinking on their own,

Dsus²
Push buttons on the phone,

Was I here once before?

Asus²
Is that my voice on the phone?

Dsus²
That last drink on my own.

E
Did I ever leave at all?

D
Confusion's familiar.

Chorus 2   As Chorus 1

Solo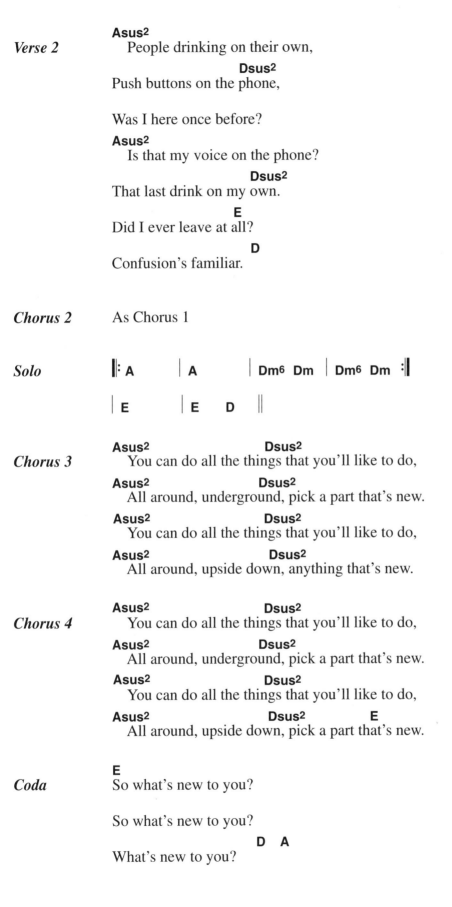

Chorus 3

Asus²   **Dsus²**
You can do all the things that you'll like to do,

Asus²   **Dsus²**
All around, underground, pick a part that's new.

Asus²   **Dsus²**
You can do all the things that you'll like to do,

Asus²   **Dsus²**
All around, upside down, anything that's new.

Chorus 4

Asus²   **Dsus²**
You can do all the things that you'll like to do,

Asus²   **Dsus²**
All around, underground, pick a part that's new.

Asus²   **Dsus²**
You can do all the things that you'll like to do,

Asus²   **Dsus²**   **E**
All around, upside down, pick a part that's new.

Coda

E
So what's new to you?

So what's new to you?

D   **A**
What's new to you?

Plastic California

Words by Kelly Jones
Music by Kelly Jones, Richard Jones & Stuart Cable

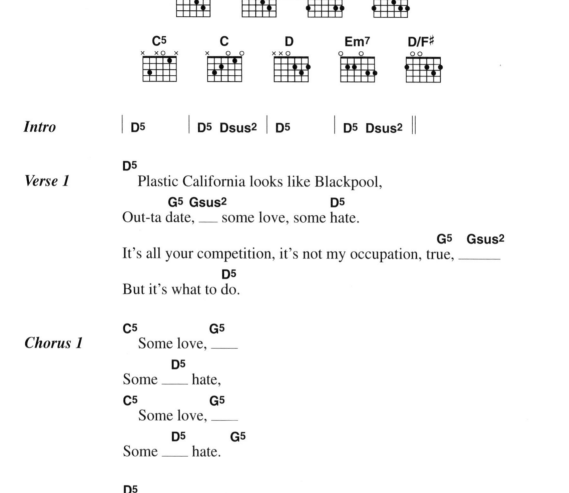

Intro | D5 | D5 Dsus2 | D5 | D5 Dsus2 ||

Verse 1

D5
    Plastic California looks like Blackpool,
   G5 Gsus2   **D5**
Out-ta date, ___ some love, some hate.

                                        G5   **Gsus2**
It's all your competition, it's not my occupation, true, _____
                   D5
But it's what to do.

Chorus 1

C5   **G5**
    Some love, ___
      D5
Some ___ hate,
C5   **G5**
    Some love, ___
      D5   **G5**
Some ___ hate.

Verse 2

D5
    I like pink architecture, flip back my red strip deck-chair,
G5 Gsus2   **D5**
Prove ___ we got nothin' to prove.

                                         G5   **Gsus2**
Gin stroke amnesia problems, overhearing talk of Hollywood, ___
          D5
We wish we could, you should.

Chorus 2

$$C \qquad\qquad G5$$
Some love, ____

$$\qquad\qquad\qquad D$$
And some ____ hate,

$$C \qquad\qquad G5$$
Some love, ____

$$\qquad\quad D$$
Some ____ hate.

‖: D | D | D | D | G5 | G5 :‖

| D5 | D5 | D5 | D5 Dsus2 ‖

Verse 3

(D5)
It's a beautiful place for nature

$$\qquad\qquad\qquad\qquad\qquad\qquad G5 \quad Gsus2$$
And all the beautiful people make it true, ____

$$\qquad\qquad\quad D5$$
You look good as you.

Chorus 3

$$C \qquad\qquad G5$$
Some love, ____

$$\qquad\qquad\qquad D$$
And some ____ hate,

$$C \qquad\qquad G5$$
Some love, ____

$$\qquad\quad Em7 \quad D/F\sharp$$
Some ____ hate.

Middle

$$\qquad\qquad G5 \quad D/F\sharp \qquad\qquad Em7 \quad D/F\sharp$$
Makes me feel great, makes me feel great,

$$\qquad G5 \qquad D/F\sharp$$
I feel new. ____

$$\qquad\qquad G5 \qquad D/F\sharp \qquad\qquad G5 \qquad D/F\sharp$$
D'ya feel new? Ha, ha. D'ya feel new? Ha, ha.

$$\qquad\qquad G5 \qquad D/F\sharp \qquad G5$$
D'ya feel new? Ha, ha,   ha, ha.

$$\qquad\qquad D/F\sharp \qquad\qquad\qquad G5 \quad D/F\sharp$$
Well I'm pleased to meet you. ____

Coda

| G5 | D/F♯ | G5 | D/F♯ |

| Em7 | D/F♯ | Gsus2 | Gsus2 ‖

‖: D5 | D5 Dsus2 | D5 | D5 Dsus2 :‖ *Play 4 times*

| D5 ‖

Roll Up And Shine

Words by Kelly Jones
Music by Kelly Jones, Richard Jones & Stuart Cable

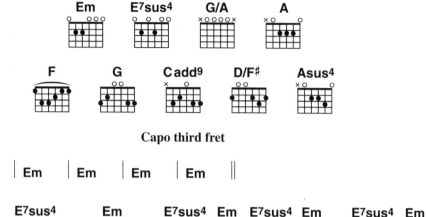

Capo third fret

Intro

| Em | Em | Em | Em ||

Verse 1

E⁷sus⁴   Em   E⁷sus⁴ Em E⁷sus⁴ Em   E⁷sus⁴ Em
Why don't you take a   look in my   mouth? _____

E⁷sus⁴   Em   E⁷sus⁴ Em E⁷sus⁴   Em
Why don't you take   a look at   yourself?

Pre-chorus 1

G/A A
So why don't you

G/A A   F   Em
Take a look around?

G/A A
So why don't we

G/A A   F   Em
Take a look inside?

Chorus 1

G   Cadd⁹ G   Cadd⁹
Roll out the shock parade,

G   Cadd⁹ G   Cadd⁹
Free-falling from a stage.

G   Cadd⁹   G   Cadd⁹
Performance and cocktails,

G   Cadd⁹ Em
Roll up and shine.

Verse 2

E⁷sus⁴   Em   E⁷sus⁴ Em   E⁷sus⁴ Em   E⁷sus⁴ Em
I hang the devil   from a circus   wire, _____

E⁷sus⁴   Em   E⁷sus⁴ Em E⁷sus⁴   Em
Face up seats, four in   love spittin'   fire.

Pre-chorus 2 As Pre-chorus 1

Chorus 2 As Chorus 1

Bridge
G   D/F♯ Asus4   G
It's time to live, lt's time to love,

    D/F♯ Asus4   G
It's time to do what's afraid of.

    D/F♯ Asus4   G
It's time to breathe, time to relieve,

    D/F♯ Em
It's time to shine. _____

Pre-chorus 3 As Pre-chorus 1

Chorus 3 As Chorus 1

Chorus 4
G   Cadd9 G   Cadd9
Bring on your shock parade,

G   Cadd9 G   Cadd9
Freaks falling   from the stage,

G   Cadd9   G   Cadd9
Performance and cocktails,

G   Cadd9 Em   G/A   A
Roll up _____ and shine. _____

Same Size Feet

Words by Kelly Jones
Music by Kelly Jones, Richard Jones & Stuart Cable

D#m7   B   E   C#m7   F#   B/D#   Esus2   Em7

Verse 1

N.C.   D#m7
A week's too long not to ring,

                                    B
Re-colours her hair and waits for him.

                                 D#m7
No cat against dog, just head over heels,

                              E
Sex twice a date, best time in years.

              D#m7
Oh no, why hasn't he phoned?

        E   D#m7
She has to wait until he's on his own,

E   D#m7
Lying and denying so nobody knows.

        E   D#m7   C#m7   B   F#
"I'll tell her this week" is what he tells her to keep her on loan.

E
   He'll buy her one day.

Link | B | B | B | B ||

(day.)

Verse 2

B   D#m7
Sex drives, oral highs, cheated wives and spies,

                                         B
Cream cakes, coffee dates, floral gifts, goodbye.

                                    D#m7
Passed away for the day, had a change of kind,

Sex change too mundane for the average mind.

E   D#m7
Oh no, she just can't see

E   D#m7
Where he is or where he's been.

cont.

    E   D♯m⁷
Looked prim and straight like she's always been,

E   D♯m⁷ C♯m⁷ B   F♯ E
All that   she   saved for went missing a-(gain.)

Link

| B | B | B | B | ‖
-gain.

Chorus 1

C♯m⁷   B
She could be, she could be, she could be ____ wrong,

C♯m⁷   B
She could be, she could be, she could be ____ wrong,

C♯m⁷   B
She could be, she could be, she could be ____ wrong,

C♯m⁷
It looks like, it looks like the word's got ('round.)

Link

‖: B | B | B | B :‖
'round.

Verse 3

(B)   D♯m⁷
They found a body in the lake,

                             B
Maybe it wasn't really his name.

                                     D♯m⁷
Same colour, same weight, same size feet,

It's the not knowing that kills you.

E   D♯m⁷
Oh no, the clock's stopped slow.

E   D♯m⁷
Every time you're on your own,

     E   D♯m⁷
You hide from the spies so nobody knows,

E   D♯m⁷   C♯m⁷   B   F♯
Scratch through the pages of a lazy day's news for a   clue,

E   (B)
Still lookin' for ____ (you.)

Link

| B | B | B | B | ‖
you.

Coda

| B | B | ‖: B | B | B | B |

| B/D♯ | B/D♯ | Esus² | Esus² :‖ Em⁷ | Em⁷ |

‖: B | B | B | B :‖ B | ‖

She Takes Her Clothes Off

Words by Kelly Jones
Music by Kelly Jones, Richard Jones & Stuart Cable

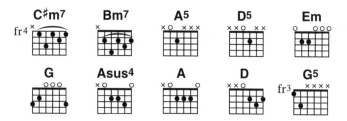

Intro | C#m7   Bm7 ||

Verse 1

A5   C#m7   Bm7
  She's got another fantasy,
A5   C#m7   Bm7
  She lives in flat number twenty-three.
A5   C#m7   Bm7
Paid first prize for carnival   queen,
A5   D5   C#m7   Bm7
  And now she takes her clothes off.

Verse 2

A5   C#m7   Bm7
  Collects the covers off of maga - zines,
A5   C#m7   Bm7
  She longs to be another teenage dream.
A5   C#m7   Bm7
  Her problem is she's turned forty - three,
A5   D5
  She still takes her clothes off.

Pre-chorus 1

Em   G   Asus4   A   D
  Got the nickname part of 'Bub - ble Joe,'
Em   G   Asus4   A   D
  They found her dead, dead as nails   at home. She said:

Chorus 1

G   D
  I'm gonna be another Marilyn,
G   D
Bleach my hair and get real thin,
G   D   A   C#m7   Bm7
  And everybody's gonna wanna dance with me.

Verse 3
```
        A5                      C♯m7  Bm7
        She loves to have a little fantasy,
        A5                           C♯m7  Bm7
        She longed to be the wife of Jimmy Dean,
        A5                      C♯m7      Bm7
        But Jimmy's head sits on Jimmy's knees,
        A5                  D5          C♯m7  Bm7
        She'd love to take her clothes off.
```

Verse 4
```
        A5                      C♯m7  Bm7
        Police are looking round at twenty-three,
        A5                           C♯m7  Bm7
        They found her hangin' from her swollen feet,
        A5                      C♯m7      Bm7
        They saw her dance last in Woolworth Street,
        A5                  D5
        She'd love to take her clothes off.
```

Pre-chorus 2   As Pre-chorus 1

Chorus 2
```
        G                    D
        I'm gonna be another Marilyn,
        G               D
        Bleach my hair and get real thin,
        G                    D            A
        And everybody's gonna wanna dance with me.
```

Coda
```
        D                A  Asus4 A  G
        Everybody's gon-na  wan - na  dance with me,
        D              A   Asus4 A    G
        Everybody wants to be      the carnival queen.
        D                A  Asus4 A  G
        Everybody's gon-na  wan - na  dance with me,
        D              A   Asus4 A
        Everybody wants to be
          G            D        A  Asus4  A
        The carnival king or    queen.
        G5              D      A  Asus4  A
        We all read the books.
        G5              D          A
        She takes her   clothes off
        Asus4 A   G
        One   by ___ one,
                D5  A  Asus4  A      G5
        One by one,      off         again.
```

45

T-Shirt Suntan

Words by Kelly Jones
Music by Kelly Jones, Richard Jones & Stuart Cable

Aadd9   A   C#m7   D   Dm   E7   G5

C   Fadd9   Am7   Bbsus2   F   Fsus2   Em7

Intro | Aadd9 | Aadd9 | Aadd9 | Aadd9 ‖

Verse 1

    A   C#m7
He was walkin' round to you,
               D
One said French afternoon,
    Dm   E7   A
So he called into a shop for two.
             C#m7
He bought himself an ice drink,
            D
A totally tropical nice drink,
    Dm   E7   A
Then he saw what he thought was you in a room.

Verse 2

             C#m7
He thought about goin' over,
            D
But you were always much older
    Dm   E7   A
And your sex-dressed breasts impressed too.
           C#m7
He'd really like to get it together
           D
Before the twelfth of never
   Dm   G5
So he's comin' over.

Chorus 1

        C   **Fadd9**
It's when all the phrases come around,

      Am7   **B♭sus2**
The clothes you wear, the sex and love.

        C   **Fadd9**   **Am7**
It's enough for the time, out-ta touch,

      B♭sus2 **F**   **G5**
Out of ———— luck.

Verse 3

  A   **C♯m7**
He always liked 'em older,

                  D
So that his top lip touched on her shoulder,

  Dm   **E7**   **A**
Lionized, undisguised, kill for you.

              C♯m7
Like to show you his tee-shirt suntan,

             D
Like to show you his minute headstand,

    Dm   **G5**
Then a gun spun open.

Chorus 2

        C   **Fadd9**
It's when all the phrases come around,

  Am7   **B♭sus2**
The clothes you wear, the sex and love,

        C   **Fadd9**   **Am7**
It's enough for the time, out-ta touch,

      F
Out of luck.

Chorus 3   As Chorus 1

Middle

G5   **Fsus2**
From you to me, to me to you,

G5   **Fsus2**
From you to me, to me to you,

Em7   **Fsus2**
From you to me, to me to you,

G5   **Fsus2**
From you to me, to me to you.

Chorus 4

          C   **Fadd⁹**
It's when all the phrases come around,

      Am⁷   **B♭sus²**
The clothes you wear, the sex and love,

        C   **Fadd⁹**   **Am⁷**
It's enough for the time, out-ta touch,

      F
Out of luck.

Chorus 5

          C   **Fadd⁹**
It's when all the phrases come around,

      Am⁷   **B♭sus²**
The clothes you wear, the sex and love.

        C   **Fadd⁹**   **Am⁷**
It's enough for the time, out-ta touch,

      B♭sus² **F**
Out of _____ luck.

      B♭sus² **F**   **G⁵**
Out of _____ luck.

A	A	C♯m⁷	C♯m⁷	
D	D	Dm	G⁵	
Aadd⁹	Aadd⁹	Aadd⁹	Aadd⁹	‖

Too Many Sandwiches

Words by Kelly Jones
Music by Kelly Jones, Richard Jones & Stuart Cable

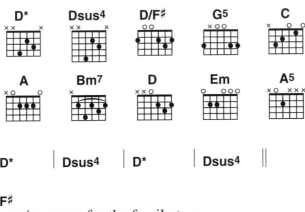

Intro | D* | Dsus4 | D* | Dsus4 ||

Verse 1

D/F♯
Shopping spree for the family tree,

G5
Haven't seen your family tree

   D/F♯   **G5**
In quite a while.

D/F♯
Too many sandwiches and wine,

G5
Sherry stains down your best man's tie,

D/F♯   **G5 C G5**
What a speech!

Verse 2

          D/F♯
The band arrive, the Granny's cry,

          G5
The singer's tongue's in the barmaid's mouth,

D/F♯   **G5**
What a voice!

D/F♯
Grandpa drunk a drop or two and,

          G5
And his head's still sunk in the portaloo,

D/F♯   **G5 C G5 D/F♯ G5**
What a man!

Chorus 1

          A   **D/F♯**
You bought a sequin dress for your chicken breast,

      A   **Bm⁷** **D**   **G⁵**   **Em**
The disco's late and he's over - paid   tonight.

        A   **D/F♯**
You got a diamond ring and a man who sings,

      A   **Bm⁷**   **D**   **G⁵**   **A**
The man who sings made love to the bar - maid twice,

                 D/F♯ **G⁵** **D** **G⁵**
And that's just tonight.

Link | **A** | **A** ||

              D/F♯
Verse 3   The blue-rinsed hairs lift up their chairs,

            G⁵
The band's too loud, they're off downstairs,

D/F♯   **G⁵**
What a noise!

            D/F♯
The bride and groom they dance their dance

             G⁵
And the singer mimes there's still a chance,

            D/F♯   **G⁵** **C** **G⁵** **D/F♯** **G⁵**
The barmaid smiles.

Chorus 2   As Chorus 1

Instrumental | **A** | **A** | **A** | **A** |

                    ||: **G⁵** | **D/F♯** | **A⁵** | **A⁵** :||

              G⁵
Bridge   Na na naa,

              D/F♯
Na na naa,

              A⁵
Na na naaa, ____

              G⁵
Na na naa,

              D/F♯   **C** **G⁵** **D/F♯**
Na na naa.

                            A   G5   D/F♯
Chorus 3   You bought a sequin dress for your chicken breast,
                          A   Bm7   D   G5   Em
                    The disco's late and he's over - paid   tonight.
                            A   D/F♯
                    You got a diamond ring and a man who sings,
                          A   Bm7   D   G5   Em
                    The man who sings made love to the bar - maid twice.

                          A   D/F♯
Chorus 4   Grandpa drunk a drop or two,
                    A   Bm7   D   G5 Em
                    Head's still sunk in the porta - loo again.
                            A   D/F♯
                    The bride and groom they danced their dance,
                          A   Bm7 D   G5   A5
                    The singer mimes there's still a chance   tonight,
                                    D/F♯   G5 D G5
                    And the barmaid smiles. _____

Coda   𝄆 A5 | A5   𝄇   *Repeat ad lib. to fade*

The Bartender And The Thief

Words by Kelly Jones
Music by Kelly Jones, Richard Jones & Stuart Cable

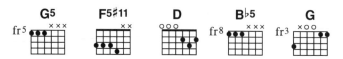

Tune bottom string to D

Intro | G5 ||

Verse 1

F5♯11
    When you think about it

                                        D
He's watching every word you say,   hey, dazed.

F5♯11
    And when he's sussed you out

He calls her up and out she comes

        D
And hustles us.

B♭5   G5   B♭5   G5   B♭5   G5
Long dig-gin', gone fish-in', love drinkin'.

Chorus 1

          D   G
The bartender and the thief are lovers,

D   G
Steal what they need like sisters and brothers.

D   G
Met in a church, a night to remember,

D   G
Robbin' the graves of bodies dismembered.

Verse 2

F5#11
He watched the lesbian talk.

                                                    D
She kissed and groped but mostly talked in lust, crushed.

F5#11
He couldn't make the call,

His eyes were gripped on licking tongues,

  D
Enough's enough, tailed for once.

B♭5   G5   B♭5   G5   B♭5   G5
Long dig-gin', gone fish-in', love drinkin'.

Chorus 2   As Chorus 1

Solo

‖: F5#11 | F5#11 | D | D :‖

B♭5   G5   B♭5   G5   B♭5   G5
Long dig-gin, gone fish-in', love drinkin'.

Chorus 3   As Chorus 1

Chorus 4

D   G
Saved what they stole to meet at the altar,

D   G
Place where they first set eyes on each other.

D   G
Flew to the sun to start life all over,

D   G
Set up a bar and robbed all the locals.

Coda

D   G
Do do do do do,

D   G
Do do do do do do do,

D   G
Do do do do do,

D   G   D
Do do do do do do do.

Traffic

Words by Kelly Jones
Music by Kelly Jones, Richard Jones & Stuart Cable

C · Am7 · Fsus2 · Am

F · Dm · Fmaj7 · G5 · Fadd9

Intro | C | Am7 | Fsus2 | C ‖

Verse 1

                            C
We all face the same way,

                 Am
Still it takes all day.

                    F
I take a look to my left,

                        C
Pick out the worst and the best.

                        Am
She paints her lip greasy and thick,

                F   Dm   C
Another mirror stare and she's going where? _____

Verse 2

                 C
Another office affair?

              Am
To kill an unborn scare?

              F
You talk dirty to a priest,

                C
It makes them human at least.

                                Am
But is she running away to start a brand new day?

        Fmaj7   Dm   C
Or's she going home, why's she driving alone? ____

Bridge 1

    F   **Dm**   **C**
Is anyone going anywhere?

    F   **Dm**
Everyone gotta be ____

    C   **Am⁷** **Fsus²** **C**
Somewhere. ____

Verse 3

                        C
She got a body in the boot,

                Am⁷
Or just bags full of food?

               Fadd⁹
Those are model's legs

                      C
But are they women's, are they men's?

                                Am⁷
She shouts down the phone, missed a payment on the loan.

                Fmaj⁷   **Dm** **C**
She gotta be above the rest, keeping up with the best. ____

Bridge 2   As Bridge 1

Solo | **G⁵** | **Fsus²** | **G⁵** | **Fsus²** | **Fsus²** | **C**   ‖

Verse 4

                   C
Wait tables for a crook

                  Fmaj⁷
Who wrote a hardback book.

                    Am
D'you teach kids how to read?

                 Fmaj⁷
Or sell your body on the street?

              C   **Am⁷**
A nurse without a job? Another uptown snob?

                  Fmaj⁷   **Dm**   **C**
But have I got you all wrong? One look and you were _ gone. ____

Bridge 3

           F   **Dm**   **C**
‖: Is anyone going anywhere? :‖   *Play 3 times*

        F   **Dm**   **N.C.**
Everyone gotta be somewhere.

Coda   ‖: **C** | **Am⁷** | **Fsus²** | **C**   :‖ *Play 3 times*